Penmanship Books
Published by Penmanship Publishing Group
593 Vanderbilt Avenue, #265
Brooklyn, NY 11238

First Penmanship trade edition: March 2014

ISBN# 978-0-9900122-4-5

Contact the author Dominique Christina
www.penmanshipbooks.com

Printed in the United States of America

THE BONES, THE BREAKING, THE BALM: A COLORED GIRL'S HYMNAL

4

The Bones

The Breaking

The Balm

THE BONES

Missing Limbs

she in the grocery store
cheaply bought woman
pullin' at the collard greens
don't put her head up for nothin".
scooped shoulders, silent.
she make me mad with how
dead she keep her mouth
she work sufferin" into bread so good it almost like
rain. like coming home. like leavin' it.
she look too much like
i used to.

i wanna tell her somethin' real
tell her somethin' 'bout the stayin'
i wanna say:
       you a six shooter baby, let one off!
       that leaves five...
       like fingers on a hand left empty
       no matter...
       you been dealin' in the deficits
       when you gon' claim that roar in your chest?
       when you gon' remember your name?
       make your blood move in concert with all that holy you got.
       red tidal right now woman
       you a swallowed mouth
       a gasp for free air
       go 'head and holler in your kitchen
       let it get in the yams and sweet bread
       let it turn your mouth over.
       cant nobody wait too long
       to get free.

My mama say, silence ain't nothin' but a wound if you hungry...

Wish I had four sets of
Hard teeth
Wish I had more bite
In me
Wish I had me a
Shovel to dig out
The quiet

To swat at the empty
To claw at the ruined city
In my throat

To be the flood...
The hurricane wind
Of LOUD

Only thing left hungry
After that kind of lifeblood storm...

The shuttered abandoned silence
I ain't content to keep.

The Dream About Being Mute

in the dream i am a swallowed mouth.
can't find my throat/
my tongue will not pull up
from her watery grave
everyone is fat from my silence/
they never stopped eating.

my stories are
small brown birds.

they do not know what love is.
they do not remember their nests.

The Dream About Shouting

in the dream every word
is red paint
i speak, it look like a murder scene.

they try shutting my lips
with caution tape

but I am burnin' my mouth down.

it's gon' come back to me
a new thing
no troll bridged tongue
no yawping
soundless empty.

in the dream
i am waiting for my mouth to be born.

when she is...

everything gon' be loud.

The Dream About Weeping

In the dream
I am fighting
My eyes.
We barter for authorship
Of the oceans I keep.

It is impossible
To keep from drowning.

The Dream About Dancing

in the dream
we are dancing
inside God
and she is laughing
new landscapes
into places we get to
together.

in the dream
you are the mountains
re-initiated into totems
I am bending over lilies healing
each tender bloom from a valley experience.

in the dream
we turn our stories
into rain

and shake the water
loose from every
leaf and tree.

The Dream about Leaving

When you are afraid
Everything is a doorway
To someplace else
So I'm tippin through my
Own impromptu life
Staring out windows
That offer too much
On the other side
My body is always betraying me.
Where I would be an
Alleyway there is always a dance floor
Where I look for an exit
Someone says: Stay.

In the dream I am
A clumsy set of hands
In my pocket.

I am epileptically scratching
For keys.

When I find them
None fit the locks.

The Dream About Stayin'g

The baby is not a gurgling coo anymore.
The house is peopled and always
A board game.

I am soaping the plates
Because it looks like commitment.

I am keeping the pots near full.

No one is hungry.

The only ache I find
Is the whirring machinery of too wild a city
Big with everything we carry

When we walk outside.

The Dream About War

"and where for men, fighting is a cause, for women, fighting is for men." -- Sylvia Plath

And I did...
Albeit folly or
Frailty
I did
Abandon my
Morality
In favor of
Biting

One wicked
Woman
Setting the
Geography
Of her soul
To stone
To yowl
Her claims
To you

When I woke up
The fight
Sat bitter
In my mouth

Like lemons

Like what I can't keep.

Dreaming of Moses

I Dreamed You Were Moses

1.
When God spoke through
That bush
His voice licking the
Flames of prophecy
I remember you
Sitting on a rock
Mouth pulled under
In wonder
Sorting sea shells
With your feet.

2.
When that sea,
(You whispered)
Red from memory
Red from want
Broke open for me,
I, inside God,
Genuflected
Inside the jubilee
Of your thighs.

The Dream About Langston

He looks like Christmas
Pomade and cinnamon
A drawn up coat and a red scarf
Laughing at Harlem
In her quixotic bricked up beauty
Leanin heavy on a stoop
Ladies askin if he's hungry
Children cussin and dribbling basketballs
Afternoon-whimsy, September sky.
It ain't cold but he keeps his coat on
He ain't stayin'
Just dropped by.

He mounts the slick pavement
Gives the big city treble
What quakes in his bones.
This is home.
This is Harlem.
An otherworldly ruckus of concrete
And blood meal
Where everything feels like dancin
Like runnin
Like keepin time with what
Ain't yours.

He pulls on the heavy air
Keeps it under his coat.

He is passing through, see?
What hunger he got now
Has no address.

A Black Girl is Not A Billboard

Rihanna,
You are a bone in my mouth.

I have tried to get you from
Around my teeth but
You, the unmovable hurt.

Oh sister for whom
The locusts come,
I been wrong to
Pretend you are not mine.

We 'sposed to
Have crow bar backbone
And blood that spills out slick as cream.

We 'sposed to know the
Devil when we see him.
He's gon' look just like our daddy
Who we ain't never laughed with.

They do not know that for
Some of us
Exit doors look just
Like trapdoors

So I see you, you terrible sister.
Sometimes we leave our ribs open
For the next big blow-

Sometimes we shake our fists and shave our heads...
Sometimes we love the lion.
Keep ourselves thin

To fit between the growl
To keep the snarling close
We test the flesh.

And call it love.

For the bones and the breaking

You gutsy bitch
Pulling at the cool night air
With the stars chanting mantras
Like negro spirituals

And you act like you don't
Know the heavy
You were born with
Your chin out over your feet
Impossible bitch
Them songs do not belong to you

All your ugly ancestry
Black and salted bone heaps
Dangling from your body
You ain't got no songs
No symphonies and
No hallelujahs
You a righteous kill

Shut them ribs up in
Your chest, I will.

You gutsy bitch.
You ugly smiling slaughter.

Ain't nobody told you how to die?

THE BREAKING

We Women of Long Memories

I was born into deliberate silence.

Where you get that howl in your bones gal?

Oh women of too much memory
What we 'sposed do with this storied flesh?

There is a holiness I am seeking.
Framed in consonants and closed fists.
The yawp of unfilled cavities.
Leave these stories in my mouth, God.
Don't let 'em run off, tail-tucked
Gon'e from me like my name be sometimes.

Let me speak 'em in resistance of history.
Let me give all them long-legged women in my lineage
Back the benefit of their belonging.
Let my longing be gristle enough to shout us back into
The scripture of our bodies.

All hail the long memoried woman.
The ones of too much marrow...
We all gathered in a photo album of sighs
Watchin' the pages turn yellow.
But I am telling the bones...
I'm tellin 'em 'til they come back to me
A new thing.

I am telling the bones...

Speak.

On the subject of long-legged women in my family...

They say when them
Two white boys
Robbed that slow moving train,
With their pistols and bad teeth
Spittle curses and wild hunger

My grandma Lizzie hid her infant son,
Swaddled and milk heavy
Under her skirt...
Cinched her knees together
And told her hands an un-trembling story.

They say when them boys
Came clanging down
The aisles
Snatching purses and pocket watches

Lizzie did not do what them other ladies did
Begging squalling yelping ladies
With their mouths pulled down
Crying *Please God* and *Do Jesus!*

She knew how to pull peach toned
Babies from her simple womb
How to stuff her skin into *please sir* and *thank you kindly*
She had not needed to be a weapon
In a long time

But they say Mama Lizzie sat there,
A long neck pushed against
An antique broach
Everything in her red and sho'nuf ready.

Come on boys
(*She thought*)
Come by here.
Know my teeth.
I got a universe
Under my skirt.
Come on boys.
I dare you.
Come *on*.

What my grandmother knew...

When you crawl out of Danville Arkansas
With a daddy that spent the
Holiday money on a banjo
With broken strings
Forcing you to eat possum for dinner
Your mama trying to
Cover the road torn flesh in
Bacon grease gravy
Crying her apologies into the
Bubbling roux
When you refuse to take a
Bite running running
For the door dipping
Under the porch
The dust congregation on
Your one good dress
The stockings would never be white again
Your daddy's hands too big to
Pull you out
You spend all night
Under the busted up floorboards
The water bugs and tics
Slip into your underwear
Put themselves in your scalp
But you won't move til morning
You'll show them
You'll show them
How wide a girl has to be
To sit in her own dark
Where no man   No man
Can reach.

Good Hair (for Najah)

It isn't unlike what Jesus had
It coils a sweet, fat yes.

My daughter sits under
A bramble bush
Pinks it up in beads
And barrettes that snap

She is already becoming
So much larger than I

Her hair a resistance movement
She is the biggest pronoun
She is the strongest verb

I watch her wrestle
With her scalp
Slick it in almond oil
With hands that look like mine
Watch her locks devour it hungrily

I touch my own more obliging hair
And think:

This girl knows how to love black
How to love it from the inside
How to hold it from a gentle place
How to put her fingers inside it
Teach it to be exactly what it is.

No more than that.

Home

It was impossible to go anywhere in Park Hill
Without walking by Granny Phifer's house
A coral peeling weathered flat
That looked like desert cake, white frosting
Awnings sugared in decay
And crab apple trees that
Spilled their fat bitter bulbs
On the lawn she religiously watered
Once in the morning
Again at dusk
Shuffling out the door in
Pink sponge rollers and corduroy
House shoes made for a man
With the heel pressed down and flat.

You could not get anywhere in Park Hill without
Going by Mr. James' barkin' ass dog
With the hind legs
Dashed pink from
Bare bone concrete backyard
Chained down pinned in
Humble fucking howl and moan realities
It took me years to call home
And Mrs. James with her unborn mouth
Making quick biscuits
Clumsy in her suffering
And too pink a lipstick shade
For her blue black stretch of skin.

If you wanted to get to the playground in Park Hill
You went by Binky and Bunky's
Red brick ranch style
Home that kept its secrets

Pushed down behind
Painted and re-painted white screen
Door with the inevitable beehive
Stuck just above it
Everything about that house had a sting.
But all fried everything all the time
Everything...neck bones, oxtails, pig's feet,
Chicken legs peppered and salted just right
Til your lips smacked wetly just to walk by
But you never just walked by
You stopped in and set your shoes
By the door
Listened for the rumble...
Said yes please to sweet potato pie...
Lost your innocence
To the sound of bacon sizzling
And maybe got your hair pressed out
If Miss Suzi felt like
Climbing into your scalp
To tackle the bramble and
Quiet your brushfire locks.

If you wanted to get to the corner store in Park Hill
You went by Richard's house...
A dude with no conscience
And no intention of coming into one
His mama was a Sunday School teacher
For the irony
You never saw his daddy he didn't have a daddy

All the worst boys in Park Hill
Didn't have a daddy

Just hands and dirty words

They slid over and around their teeth
'Til they could spit 'em at you in your gym shorts
And rubber shoes and occasional
Hair beads and barrettes.

You could not get anywhere in Park Hill
On Saturday mornings without
Duckin' from Jehovah Witnesses
Early morning like so damn early
Like too fuckin early
Door knockin' and God hustlin'
Pamphlet-heavy chics in pastels peddling
Redemption with no real road map
Cuz it meant you couldn't cuss the way
You would need to
So you hid behind the curtains
'Til they left, watched 'em go
To the next house and not get in there either
They didn't never get in...
And maybe that's why The Lord
Couldn't find you quick enough

Cuz you were duckin' down
And hidin' out even from yourself
But it would take you years
To know that
So for now your days
Are street lights
And local gangs and
When they came on and
When they shut down...

If you wanted to have your first kiss in Park Hill
You did so deliberately
In the alley behind that one nasty girl's

House whose mama smoked Camels
And was never home to
Catch her daughter doin' nothin'...

You pursed your lips out
Leaned into your galloping want
And waited for a messy exchange
That would send saliva
Down your jawbone
But you wore eyeliner after that...

And thought you knew what a woman was
Thought you knew you wanted to be one...

Back alleys are not the right places
For that kind of clarity
But you held onto it anyway
Because that's what you do
When there's nothing else to hold.
When there's nowhere else to go
When the place you are is the only
Thing telling you what you will become
You hold onto it
And call it home.

Because what I should do is move to Brooklyn...

The swooshing metal
Of the articulated city is an anthem
Sweet land of liberty sashay all
Slick footed and,
So whatchu know about freedom, delicious...

And I could live here.

In the honeyed grit of Brooklyn
Pull my hips around
The bricks and moan just
Like they do and
They do moan and bleat
When them corner boys make everything
Feel like an ambulance ride
And girls be hard like
What candy your grandmama kept in
Her pocketbook that you could only have
If you sat up straight and
Tucked all the wild in.
Kept it pressed down flat and neat
'Til the street lights
Flickered you some brand new thing
To bet on or bleed to or
Sweat under...

I could live here

Slap my hands down 'round
Every ticking clock and be my mama's daughter
All morning
Laughing a red ripe laugh and
Swooping down on my used to be life

To catch it by the ankles
And pull it underneath this city, fat with
Music and shimmy
Like razor blades,
Like a twirling skirt,

To be a girl again.

A Hot Thing

When I come back
Next time
I'm gon' be a fat wet
Mewling thing
Scratchin' at your back.
Some nasty woman howl
Laid low in your bed.
My rollicking slick
My coiling pink
You can't get too far
From the sound
Of my flesh
I be a fat wet
Mewling thing
A nasty woman
Staining your sheets
Like God know something
'Bout shudder and
My music-making hands
Like He done loosed
Me unto your
Midnight porch
Lappin' night sky
Up under my thin skirts
Maaaaaaan
Ain't no heaven like
A woman

No hell neither.

A Pretty Thing...

With stones for teeth
She ate dirty rice and vanilla wafers
Cussed boys for hogging the tire swing
And stitched up her spine
'Til it reached a hot point.

No rooms in the house were big enough.

She was the first time
I heard the word "cunt"
A playground epithet

That sat in my mouth like coal.
She could not stay in private school.

No money and no rooms were big enough.

They say her boyfriend
Was the meanest kind.
A bricked up snarling nasty.
He killed her on a Wednesday.

She had pushed out of a training bra
Grew thick flesh like
Butter on a hot spoon
Still cussed the boys and swatted
Them down.
He did not like her mouth

How it shook with embers

How it tasted like something burning
Like blood fruit
Like a slaughterhouse

Where no rooms were ever big enough.

For Neambe

And so you squattin' down under
a clanging life with too loud
a man in it,
look around and
all your parts are scattered
'cross the living room
like you forgot what dancin' felt like
and it takes you so many mornings
to collect all the broken syllables
in your name,
each mishandled moment
that made your bones sit in your body
like canons,
like war,
like thrumming from the inside wouldn't eventually kill you,
like your mama didn't tell you
bout your magic BEFORE you struck
a match between her thighs.
and now all you know
is your shut mouth.
don't have enough teeth
to chew through the
bloody stumped memories.
you want to climb the sky but
can't find your throat no place
everything is a bottled up capture
can't no light get inside
the way you love
cuz you love like a lynchin' rope,
like a wound,
like a dead thing,
like a broad stroke,

you love like a trench,
gobblin' up the night...
lawd your own sunken self
is peekin' up
through bolted door
wantin' to know somethin'
bout the outside
if you could get your limbs back
if you could get your limbs back...
you could get up...
you might could get free.

ShapeShifter Woman

I come to things dawn-dew slick
I make morning slide into me..
Open my mouth and sing
You my teeth...
They are totems of stories
You're listening for.

Do you know what happens
When a woman becomes
An ache?

Everything is Sassoon in her.

To love her is to slip the
Wilderness under your tongue.
Catch the thorn-drunk sound
Of her shiftin' better than weather.

She can look like you like it, man.
Watch her look like you like it man.

Watch her be an empty drawer in the kitchen.
Watch her be a bread basket full to bursting.

Kaleidoscopic slick-handed changeling woman.

You can't know her
She too clever for that...

The Journey Woman

"Where you runnin' off to girl? You leave before you enter..."

an entrance don't coo
like an exit.

it ain't a better ballroom
than a highway, a dirt road...
some far off unknown place.

i keep hearin' the hills
say: *come dance girl*
and my feet go lookin'
for them songs
what's the use in bein' still
with so much world
to pirouette in?

i wanna get it all over me
the soot and sparkle of
a thousand cities
hot late nights
in the thick of nowhere

my bones don't do
nothin' for me
when I'm sittin' still

so I be runnin'
these feet to wildfire
sashay shimmy stomp
and slide on down

i'm a Saturday night
every mornin' baby

pullin' up sunsets
i ain't seen

don't look for me
to stay baby...

i'm already gone...

The Conjure Woman
"You got so much magic girl...you thick with it."

unbraided conjure woman
lookin' for wind...
you ain't no ordinary anything.

they keep lookin' for you
to duck under all those stories
those lonesome hooked mouth
tellin' lies stories
bout you bein' small
enough to chew through.
the words gon' drop on your feet
like a stillbirth
like a dead thing

everything they ever said
was a hollow place
to hide your body in

but you?
you keep growin' too big for holding down
they can't get the nails in just right

you a magic thing.
keepin' lemon balm and lightning bugs.

your sharp straight neck
your biting teeth.
your un-split womb
your mud-struck life
you a *dance* conjure woman
your knuckles shook loose
your pushed out knees

you a slow sizzle conjure woman.

an old thing
no kin and no promise
of heaven.

Ghost Woman

They will say you are a story
Nobody has business believin' in
What with Jesus and integration

How the midnight caterwauling
Is some far off whistling train
They couldn't catch if they wanted to...

And they don't want to.

They would rather watch the sun
Be swallowed up by God
Than to imagine you back
And creeping low 'round the basement
Shooing birds out the attic.

You are an unwanted visitor
A locked door that won't stay closed.
The hinges creak and
We are an abandoned church.
A faithless vacancy
Knocks in our chests

We don't like a goodbye
We scared of resurrection.

Ghost Woman, if you can come back...
In your dirt-bitten don't nobody want you
Bloodless body
If you can come back hissin' through the floor boards
Grindin' your teeth,
If you can come back
Bringing the cold dead air...

Who can't?
Oh lord...
Who can't?

The Third Eye Woman
"She sees it. She sees it. She sees it."

I can't tell you how I knows it.

Seem like lightnin' strikes on the inside
And I go tremblin'

Seem like I can't stop the stories

They slide down
They slip in

I can't shake em no how
It ain't no regular dream
It ain't no picture stuck in the frame
It ain't no song you know the words to

It an old thing
It a new thing
It a thing comin' on

Comin' on
Comin' on

Sometimes I shuts me eyes to it
But something stays open
The god witch part

Keeps on bringin' in the
Stories I ain't wrote
They push my eyeballs loose
Like gawd playin' marbles
In my skull

I say BE STILL and TURN ME LOOSE
But they keeps a earthquake shook
In the eye I can't close...

Wonder will it work when I'm dead...

The Rebellious Woman

Two fists be how she worship.
She a rooftop hollow point
Clear of soul
The plural biting hand.
See her.
The paradoxical bitten
Apple the swollen
Veins a clipped chuckle at
The throat.
She done made the word *no* a religion.

"...Sinnerman where you gonna run to?"

Go to the rock. Pour your own succulent everything into her, stir.
A rock, is a deliberate pulpit. She thirsty for the wind in your body.
For the sticky tender meat. When you a whistlin' flame glowin'
dangerous, the rock. Swallow six gallons of her secrets, the rock.
She tellin' you what you forgot you knew. Set it next to your scarlet
heart. Your heart, a bruised red house for holdin' things. Ain't no
way to keep your breast milk without swallowin' gasoline. You was
assembled from reaction. An afterthought by way of rib. You could
be a mountain, a StoneHenge girl of ruin. 'Cept you run when you
'sposed to strut. What hilltop you know ever apologize to the ones
who caint climb it? The spell worker's heart is a *ritual*. Go to the
rock. Split the earth hard and quick. Be the monster and the magic
if it let you keep your skin. You gon' bleed before it is done.

Hard to put a hand on it.

The way we so fluent
in our sufferin',
the way we soak in it,
'til it hangs on,
'til we in a bad luck way.

I don't know 'bout you
but I got low so many times
my heart ran out...
like the silly bitch i tried to be
just ran *out* and left lookin'
for a place to plant things/
things that don't wither so quick
or droop so low
just sad.

a girl can be a footnote you know.
she can take all the meaning
out of her own story
give it to some undeserving fool
who buys the wrong kinda bread
and don't never say thank you
for how wet she can still get...
though loveless.

Hard to put a hand on it.

But I gave up dyin' a long time ago.
soon's I realized I ain't got but one
kinda heart.
the kind that keeps the ache
but don't wanna make a home of it.

the kind that keeps bubblin' its sugar
in a blackgirl, torrential
but tryin'.

I tell her about Jasper Texas...

It's like this, (I say),
There is a road in
Jasper Texas,
That dreamed it was a wolf,
It practiced a wild hunger.
It waited on an offering.
Sees James Byrd and sharpens the teeth.
The white boys feed the road.
They laaaaaugh and spill
Their beer.
The foam sits in their whiskers
Puddles under their feet and
The asphalt drinks what it can...

Becomes the spine bone circus
The tail bone scrape
The razored elbow
The ripping skin
Whatever was pink inside
Whatever thrummed
Whatever pulsed
Got a good dragging
Miles and miles of bone meal
The road was a wolf.
It knew it had been.
The white boys baying
At the dawn limp moon

James Byrd can't hush the burning.
He is pulled behind the pickup truck
The chains biting ankle bone to shrapnel.
He is trying to latch his chin to his chest
He can hear his daddy tell him

Keep your head, man. Keep your head.
He is *trying.*
The white boys don't stop
The blood letting.
It is their favorite kind of music.
A ticker tape of soft tissue
They hit a culvert,
The steel pipe crescendo...
And the all over heat
Went out.
The road licked the severed limbs clean.
The blood bone ritual
Of unholy.

The white boys bayed at the moon.
They laaaaaughed and spilled
Their beer.
The foam settled in their whiskers.

This is how you talk politics in Texas.
A chain.
A black boy.
A bludgeoning.

Sekia's Killer

Girl. You fit inside your body like your heart been broke.
I ain't sayin' I'm best for you but
I do got plans witcho hips in mind
You mighty pretty this evenin'
Dressed in yo best distractions
Lips parted like you know you gon'
Always be hungry
Let me fill you up girl
Lean legs is scripture to a nigga like me

Where you goin' where you goin' where you goin'?
You ain't gon' be beautiful when you get there
Forget that business
What you need with freedom girl?
That ain't a word a man made up
Thinkin 'bout you.
That's a pioneer's word.
A hunter's word.
A warrior's word.
It ain't for you witcho silly biology
Click-clacking 'cross the pavement
Like you got somewhere to be.
Bitch I'ma give you a place to be.
Laid up under me with a scowl on yo face
Wonderin' bout love and how come you can't never find it.
Where you goin' where you goin' where you goin'?
What you mean you don't want me?
What you mean you don't want US?
You see me standin' here tryna give you a Saturday night?
You think I can't get a woman to part for me?
You think I need you?
You think you better than me?
You ain't the first bitch I wanted to kill

But you the one I put down reaaaaaaal easy
You see this blade I got?
It's gon' dance you to right to sleep
Tits be like blood fruit.
Runnin a red river goodbye
Down the sewage drain.
I like you a lopsided star
I like you a right angle stretch
Yeah...this way...
I like you better this way.

The Shug Avery Mimicry

she say I be lookin too hard with all my eruptin' *"woo chile"* smoke
signals turned *up* baby you don't know? a red dress and a white
feather *hey now!* shakin' my Shug Avery everything 'til the lights go
out I come in as the loudest church bell the tickin' boom the silk
purse all over see through licorice lips and red letter prophecy ain't
no end to this party I got pitched between my thighs why you think
The Lord made Eve it ain't the apple it's the *snake* the dangerous
knowing the drippin' fruit baby you don't know? she say you
lookin' too hard soon somebody gonna want what you got you
gon' have to give it men don't say please women lay down and go
empty til he finish the plunder and slips out without so much as
thank you but I been a dead thing dust cluttered and unborn I been
a explanation and a steady apology but don't nobody get to sing til
you try on your mouth put your hip bones into exhibition naw I
done tried to let go of glimmer but what I got after that? an old
sofa an unmade face a worry too many nights with no rebellion
make me wanna curse my own sugar naw I be lookin' hard like
men do pretending I can't feel the mother wit like I don't know a
softer way baby you don't know? ain't but one way to dance openly
if you a woman, it's a red dress and a white feather a *come on over*
and a *don't get close*...I erupt baby...I erupt.

The Sula Mimicry

Some of us gon' be wicked
So you can know God better.
Do you know what kind of
Stone a woman needs
To watch a drowning?
To see the boy sputter, go under
And keep still?
To witness her own mama's dress catch fire?
To be close enough to smell the sizzling flesh
And not move?
The gristle you need
To permit the sacrifice?
To deal only in your own flesh?
To make no other promises to the world?
What is grief but an ill-fitting dress?
Some sagging at the knees pair of trousers
You can't run in...
I can leave the bottom
But I come back
With a worldly haul,
The white men I rode
The head-hunting mistress yeah...
I come back and
Pull your husband underneath me
So what?
Make your moans sound
Like an un-chiming clock.
He don't worry about time with me.
I don't say sorry.
I ain't sorry.
Some of us gon' have to be wicked.
So y'all can huddle together

And pray.
Some of us gon' have to be wicked.
So y'all can huddle together...

And pray.

Rachel Jeantal (Trayvon Martin's friend)

They lookin' at me like MY mouth don't work.
Like it got too many teeth
Like my bones big for breakin'
They eyes be Do Not Enter signs full-a shriek

> *Black bitch witcho pressin comb ugly*
> *All yo inconvenient flesh*
> *Spillin out in the newsreels like you*
> *Got a story we should hear*

You don't conjugate right they
Say you a lie
My underbite mean
I need a boot in my mouth
You go down a road at night
You too black and nearby...
You a thief that need killin

The rain make you suspicious
Yo hoodie make you suspicious

You walk too fast you wrong
You walk too slow you wrong
You black you wrong you wrong you wrong.

They don't know how old they is to me...

I grew up with *die bitch* stories
They can't never come quiet
Can't sneak up on no nigga like me
Can't sneak up on no nigga period
We so full of bite back and wild eye hungry

We ain't got no God
We aint got no country
We a righteous kill
We bleed delicious

We don't belong no place
The ground lick our bones

Shoot 'em again
Kill em right

Say we gold teeth thugs, unholy
Say we shifty
Say we puddled over in drugs
The housing project circus freaks
You can pulp cuz God don't love us
Who can love the ocean floor?
I know what it be like
To talk to a dead boy
To hear him before he slip from his skin
To know he bein chased bein watched
To hear the wolf gnash his teeth in the background
To hear a black boy say he runnin'
To hear him say he ain't runnin' no more
How many of us you tryna kill, huh?
How long you gon' keep yo post-reconstruction
Stop and frisk nasty?
How long before you point yo gun
At another one George?
You got the taste of it now ain't you?
You like the gated community genocides.
The lickety-split shudder of a black boy
Cryin' mercy
Cryin' for his mammy
Cryin' for help in a dark that wanna keep him

Wanna shake loose his bones
Wanna handle him harsh
Wanna see the shrapnel sizzle
Through soft tissue

You so old to me.
I ain't scared a you.
You hear me George?
You a million murder stories
A million bodies
Mass grave massa.
New world police
Same old coward
Same old cowboy
Same old hot hand
Same old lynch rope
Same old laws
Same old courtroom
Same old jury
Same old outcome

You a Jim Crow post card
A new suit and a old lie
I ain't scared a you
But you want me to be.

> *Shoot 'em AGAIN.*
> *Kill 'em right.*
> *Do it good this time.*
> *Make him squeal.*
> *Stop his heart.*
> *He a righteous kill.*
> *When he's gone don't fret.*
> *There's gon' be another.*

There's gon' always be another.
Shoot 'em again.
Kill 'em right.

Kill 'em all.

THE BALM

Mahogany Browne

The afternoon we got drunk on
Margaritas and
Heavily abridged Mexican food
And you bought me a book
With a hurricane in it,

And the frequent desperation
Of sunlight sizzled through
Our shitty waiter and
Our long skirts...
And we drank the salt
And swallowed the lime
And talked about white women

Away from the wet feet of New York City
Where Brooklyn splits open
To suck down the drunken gossip
And we were a new country of
Black girl sugar
Swinging our feet
Like linen hanging out to dry
And row upon row of
Crooked gapped tooth buildings
Pretty with sudden spring...

And we, colossal enough,
To know that moment had a life inside it

A wet laughing stretch of:
You big, baby.
You big.

Philadelphia where she is and I am not...

Stranded in the   center of
A landlocked longing
     Each night my
Fingers become tentacled
     And slick from reaching
It is a silly little dance
     Trapped in these un-christened bones
On my porch sometimes
     I fold myself into
What I remember of her voice
     Distract myself looking for wind
But she is under my rib cage now
     A sudden love
A persistent gust
     In my chest
I am heroic in my affection.
     Want to lay down my daily self for her
Want to spin a soft black song for her
     Want to climb into her skin
Memorize the tulip bulb atoms
     Shudder along the soft lines
Of her insides
     Til she know how fat and strong
In possibility we are.
     How symbolic do we need to be?
She is home to me.
     A beautiful beckoning
Of moonlit limbs and
     Vulnerability stretching
Itself out deliciously and
     We are the best thing about our bodies
Spilled and dripping with
     Want I am clamoring for her

70

I would wait for generations.
Die and come right back like Lazarus
To slip my fingers in her skin one more time...
For her...

Because it does not matter anymore not anymore and not ever again

that there were men with too many teeth
cluttering up my used-to-be self
'til she bled and broke
a lopsided and uncelebrated bit of flesh
too many long bones to chew through
to ever be called by own name.

and it does not matter anymore not anymore and not ever again
that i grew my own fangs and body, glittered blood
til everyone who tried to love me
had to taste every howl
couldn't keep my
mouth closed against inherited secrets
so i bit and clawed and closed.

naw it does not matter anymore not anymore and not ever again
that i still keep every ugly anything that has ever
happened to me in the next room
visit them in the winter...
standing in the doorway of my own awful everything
fill my fists with shrapnel
hold it up to the light
laugh into every wound
and remember that NONE of it killed me
that ALL of it could have.
i just stand there...i stand right there shouting:

hey! i see you Ed and Brian and Gerald and Leo, Uncle Junior,
Cillento and Roger and Raymond! i see you.
suburban werewolf ugly.
I see you alcoholic rapacious father of two braided daughters.
magnolia scented brown girls who broke in just the right way.

it was familiar music to bleed to.
to suffer the feet to a calloused forever limp.
i see you step daddy bump in the night
persistent ghost.
it's been thirty years since your skin slipped from your bones
and I am still inviting you into things to pull at the hem of my
prettiest skirts.
am I the ghoul of a girl you wanted?
is my memory the way I keep killing myself?
how many times do I need to kill myself?
but it does not matter anymore not anymore and not ever again
how modest a moon I can be
how midnight is a howl across my cheek...

any memory that tells me I am ugly
is a liar I know how to kill.
any memory that tells me I am damaged
is a liar I know how to kill.
any memory that tells me I died in childhood
is a liar I know how to kill.
you ugly worthless awful yesterday everything.
i do not fuck my lover with your name on my lips.
i do not hold her wondering why she is wet and perfect and with
me.

you ugly worthless awful yesterday everything.
i love her because I am whole.
i am full of something real.
a woman with so much wilderness left
one day I will not mention you at all.
one day it will not be a fight.
one day all the rubble will leave this body.

A Love Song

So Dominique crackles down from her Himalayan perch
To wander and wait for winter's slow reply to dreaming.
And finds instead a girl who has shaken loose
Every autumn leaf under the jaundiced eye of a sun
That hangs deliciously like a quartered orange
Pineapple in the eternal limbs of a wind-fresh
Pale blue sky.

She wishes for war.
Wants to shut out the sudden un-authored incandescent
Faith-making music of her smile but she came in this way.
emerged warm-rain dripping and shiny from her mother's
Starry night womb sleepy eyed. Grinning.
A hunger in the belly and the bones.

She is making me a world.
One that is not the work of some desperate architect
Whose cruel design calls for blood spatter on the masonry.
There are bridges here, women with mango in their mouths
Singing through pulp men with dirty faces and perfect teeth
Dancing on tabletops and everywhere there are children
Whose bodies will always only be their own
No snatching hands no neglected bloated bellies
No forever famine...just wind and the flapping of wings.

She is making me a world.
Her guitar picked poetry and quiet confessions
Her long storied limbs, the bruised blue muscle of memory
The girls who brought misery, the clutched and heaving
Alleyways in heart and thump
That have moaned and rocked what she was
When she was not herself
Into long sighs of dis- remembrance

She is the reason these hands still matter.
The rocking of boats.
The keeper of wind.
Symphonic praise and reluctant prayer

She is boarding up the old buildings I died in.
Licked to cinder in the songs she makes up
And I am loving her widely from here.
Have abandoned the citizenry of the always certain.
We are giddy and sugar-drunk exhilarated
Poised on the brink of far-flung
Secret kisses that wet our
Pink basin mouths to hymns.
We are sky-seeking and looking for
Wind in the un-resounding streets
That have not learned to
Keep their silences to themselves.

My head swells ponderous with gathered love syllables
To be pushed into her marrow.

This is world making.
A dusky orange sun dance of bodies and bottomless frivolity.

Let me love her forever God.
Let her know the unblessed pages in my notebook.
Let me cast off the gray grit dark matter days that counted
themselves into Insignificance because she had not yet shown up.

Let everyday be another open windowed
Drafty afternoon lost to the tangle of flesh.

Let her know.

We can devoutly worship the whimsy of this thing.
Can bask and frolic in the whimsy of this thing
Can leap and stretch in the whimsy of this thing.

The vivid colors of a remembered connection.
Saliva trails on the neck.
Weather whipped bones settling in around the fire
Of hip bone and physics.

And I am five states over writing love poems.
What a giddy bit of business.
So make me a world, girl.
I will be coming as myself.
Make me a world.
And when you're done...
We should lie down.

Another love song...

today, in a city that cannot pronounce my name
in a bookstore made up mostly of old lady
crooked limbs arthritic grasps for Louis Lamour books
marked down and stuffed in wicker baskets
lining the sidewalk leading up to the store
baring the declarative pumpkin and scarecrow motif...
everything is orange and replete with crocheted
bookmarks sewn committedly by some local artisan and
i am the only black girl around.
ain't no anomaly in that.
i know how to be lonely in places like this one...
that serve grits with everything and keep their scabbed over stories
left out for anybody to thumb through.

i am in a town that cannot pronounce my name
and will not try and the lamp posts, the painted over rail cars,
the silences big enough to die in, the whistle stop cafes,
the one big building in the center of town
with the chiming clock...the perpetual cock's crow..
(somebody's Christ is always bein crucified in places like this)
all tell me how far from her i am.

i am in a bookstore with old ladies frosted pink with talcum
powder.
they creakin' through the aisles
lookin' for cookbooks with recipes that
wont aggravate the diabetes they got or the
high cholesterol they had.
and i am distracted by the whole damn thing.

by the cowboys in their ironic hats and Levi's
smelling of pine oil with mud on their boots...

and the talcum powder puffed ones
and the scavenged basketfuls of discount Louie Lamour books
and the way everything here looks like an evacuation...
a place where the wilderness is kept.

i am in a city that cannot pronounce my name and will not try.

and the person i love is five states away.
the desperation is almost delicious.

and the talcum'd ladies and the
cattle rustlers and the discount books are not her.
the sugar dimpled baby dangling
prettily from his mama's ample hips is not her.
the boy at the front desk is not her.
the song i heard on the radio,
which sounded to me
like my own wailing, is not her.
the journal I bought because
it is the color of love letters burning is not her.
my memories of her are not her.
none of it is her.

i am a continent of forest fires.
my breasts, two irreligious totems glowing red.
i am five states away and it feels like Armageddon.
feels like clamoring for a kiss.
like an empty sugar bowl.
like a toothless grin.
like a song I can't remember.
like a dance I do not know.

look how heavy and alive we are.
i'm gon' make my way home to her.
open my mouth like waiting for communion.

spill into her hungry...
put my fingers on that one raised vein
that grins through her skin just under her ear.
paint her neck with my mouth,
it is wet and wide like me...
yeah. tomorrow i go home.
because that is where she is
because she is an atlas

because she calls me into my body
and pronounces every syllable of my
every moan in my
every shimmy in my
holy and sometimes unmentionable...

name.

Here and there and everywhere now

You are finding these fragile rooms
That are wedged in my chest like
Every other forgotten unsung thing
About me and bringing them out
To dance.
We are a ballroom of sequins and sex.
The secrets we are no longer willing
To keep have fizzled down to
Slick paste. We put it on everything.
Laugh at the mess and do it again.
This morning I remembered how
Much of me I am.
The way I have distilled to
Wetness on your collarbones,
Under your fingernails...
How I hope you will not wash it off
Until you are certain that those things
Tell you about fifty years from now
When we are mostly right angles
In a kitchen with peaches stuck in sugar jars
A bowl of plums souping over on the table,
I am making lime jello
Because it looks like commitment.
How I promised this moment when we
Were young and thin from hunger
How lime jello and peach preserves
Are sometimes the only promises that matter...
How your hands will hold more tremble
How my hips will sometimes creak
How there will be more of us to consider...

Here and there and everywhere now
We have stopped window shopping our dreams

We are holy and fucking forever
If we choose it.
I will always be foul mouthed.
You will never be a vegetarian.

I will obsess about coffee brands and
You will indulge it because I never let go of your hand.
We are walking down the grocery aisle
Snarling at products that are not
Grown right or packaged well
We will always be an open mouthed kiss
Always long bones reaching for what
Sounds like music
We will crane our necks into
The space we occupy and call it home.
You will always be my home.

It is fifty years from now and we are still silly flirtation
Still the occasional shyness and quiet.
You will still be trying to keep me organized.
I will slap at your hands because fuck organization.
I will be making lime jello
And singing Billie Holiday songs in your ear
My voice will have changed by then.
It will sound like a rainstorm
We can make love through.
This life is a rainstorm
We can make love through.

You are going to do my hair in our kitchen.
It will be a rainforest for your hands to get stuck in.
I will not mind it much.
It will be gray and impossibly everywhere
I will have grown it to thick tufts of tangle and exclamation

You will quiet your trembling hands while braiding.

Here there and everywhere now...
We are lucky and winged and exactly like this.
The old walloped loneliness of before
Is just chronology..
Smaller numbers of a when
Whose math no longer matters.

When I pray now I seek your face.
The mentioning of your name
Is how God finds me.
I will never be lost again.

This is the nature of prayer.
To utter the name of your beloved in the dark
To dance with them in the light

To promise the lime sunrise and mean it.

Because Crushes are Sometimes More...

I write love poems as myself.
A woman composed mostly
Of labyrinths.
There are a few of us left.
Slick fingering our crystal ball cervixes
Into children who will tell all our secrets.
We seem unreal.
Worth a million last night rituals
Dressed in longing.
Tied to the whole damn world
In impressionistic fragments and wide hipped
Unclaimed hallelujahs.
I want to know the praise shout of your mouth
When it is a dark and howling tunnel
Painting nighttime on my neck.
I want to pull you under. Be a caterwauling yawp
In a long red skirt.
Crane your neck into this storied flesh
And catch the ache in my thighs.
What a bloody mishmash of want.
What a slapstick comedy of bodies and skin
Smacking messily into each other
A good rumble.
Come and find me famished.
Do not let these bones stretch across
An unclaimed geography of midnights.
A quivering atlas of collar bone and teeth.
This is a dangerous knowing.
Here God barters for the rights to
Every moan.
Let me stretch myself dizzily along the
Sound of your flesh.

Let me grow what gardens I can.
Part your lips and let my name rest easy there
The spell workers heart is a ritual.
Look at the wildlife in these limbs.
We are mostly exultation.
Dancing on the edge of the world.
A smoke stack.
A deep well.
A good rumble.

Dominique Christina is a writer, performer, educator, activist, and mother to four wildly expressive children who do not use inside voices, ever. She holds four national titles in the three years she has been competing in slam, including the 2012 Women of the World Slam Champion and 2011 National Poetry Slam Champion. Dominique has over 10 years of experience as a licensed teacher, holding double Masters degrees in Education and English Literature from the University of Arkansas. She believes words make worlds. She is making a world. This is her first book. Her second, *Writing In Fire,* is set for publication in Fall 2015 with SoundsTrue Publishing.

THANK YOU

My gratitude is all over everything. It's running into everything. So thank you. Thank you to my mama, Professor Jacquelyn Benton, who has always embodied impossible magic and beauty of womanness, thank you to my big sister Lisa Marie who keeps her back straight period, to my children: Salih, Najah, Amir, and Igi, who try really hard to keep their voices down when I am writing and who give me things to write about, and to Faatma who is the truest kind of artist and the best kind of friend, and to Ayinde Russell who is brilliant and honest and who holds safe space for me, to Rachel McKibbens who keeps my secrets and gives me the kind of hope I didn't think I could have, and to la milagra Denice Frohman who I love and who saved me, and finally to the mighty Mahogany L. Browne, the widest example of black girl juju, her depth of heart and sisterhood redeems.

Penmanship Poets

Anthology	Toss the Earth: Poems That Move Us
Ken Arkind	Coyotes
Ashley August	Licorice
Mahogany L. Browne	Swag
	Dear Twitter: Love Letters Hashed Out On-Line
Michael Cirelli	Everyone Loves the Situation
William Evans	In the Event You Are Caught Behind Enemy Lines
Adam Falkner	Ten for Faheem
Barbara Fant	Paint, Inside Out
Falu	10 Things I Want To Say To A Black Man
Eboni Hogan	Grits
Chinaka Hodge	Mirrors in Every Corner
Zora Howard	Clutch
Tonya Ingram	Growl & Snare
Ishmael "Ish" Islam	Meet At Greene
Dasha Kelly	Hershey Eats Peanuts
Carvens Lissaint	The Inspiration From: Heart To: Page
Justin Long-Moton	Manual
Aja-Monet	Black Unicorn Sings
Shappy Seaholtz	Spoken Nerd Revolution
Danez Smith	Hands On Ya Knees
Jaha Zainabu	The Corners of My Shaping
Lauren Zuniga	The Nickel Tour

www.Penmanshipbooks.com